ICT TRADING STRATEGY FOREX

The Inner Circle Trader, ICT Kill zones, ICT Order flow, Fair value gap (FVG), Change of Character (ChoCh) And Risk Management

Mark M. Darby

ICT TRADING STRATEGY FOREX

All rights reserved. No part of this publication may be reproduced, distributed, or transmitted in any form or by any means, including photocopying, recording, or other electronic or mechanical methods, without the prior written permission of the publisher, except in the case of brief quotations embodied in critical reviews and certain other noncommercial uses permitted by copyright law.

Copyright © Mark M. Darby 2024

ICT TRADING STRATEGY FOREX

TABLE OF CONTENTS

Chapter 1: Inner Circle Trader..5
    What Is Inner Circle Trader? 5
    Implementing ICT Strategies Into Practice for Improved Market Understanding 8
    ICT Components 10
    Factors Affecting ICT Trading 12
Chapter 2: ICT Killzones..16
    Meaning of ICT Killzone 16
    The Four ICT Killzones..18
    The Asian Range Killzone 18
    The London Open Killzone 19
    Characteristics of London Killzone 20
    The New York Open Killzone 21
    Characteristics of New York Killzone 22
    The London Close Killzone 23
    Characteristics of London Close Killzone..............24
    Importance of ICT Killzones to Forex Traders.......25
    Identifying ICT Killzones..25
    Optimization and Risk Management 27
Chapter 3: Order Flow 29
    Order Flow Trading: What is It? 29
    The Difference Between Order Flow Trading And Other Types Of Trading..31
    How Does Order Flow Trading Work? 32
    Basics of Order Flow Trading 36
    Advantages of Using Order Flow Strategy 39
Chapter 4: Fair Value Gap..41
    FX Fair Value Gap...41
    Measuring Fair Value Gap 42

How Fair Value Gap Forms 44
How to Trade the Fair Value Gap 46
Advantages and Disadvantages of Fair Value Gap 48
Additional Tips For Fair Value Gap 49
Chapter 5: Change of Character CHoCH 51
How to Use ChoCh in Trading 52
How to Identify ChoCh 53
Chapter 6: Risk Management and Control 57
ICT Forex Trading: Avoid Common Errors and
Maximize Profitability 57
Increasing Earnings in ICT Forex Trading 61

ICT TRADING STRATEGY FOREX

Chapter 1: Inner Circle Trader

What Is Inner Circle Trader?

A notion or person within the trading sector who makes claims to possess unique information or tactics that might result in profitable trading results is referred to as an "Inner Circle Trader" (ICT), especially when it comes to Forex trading.

The Inner Circle Trader, Michael J. Huddleston, is credited with popularizing the phrase by providing instructional information on trading principles, market analysis, and tactics that are said to provide traders an advantage in the financial markets. ICT aims to give a comprehensive trading education by focusing on a variety of themes, including price action, market structure, and the mental aspects of trading.

Three Things to Know:

- Michael J. Huddleston invented the Inner Circle Trader system, which goes by the acronym ICT.

- Its main goal is to comprehend market psychology and the role of institutional participants.

- ICT uses a broad strategy that includes a timeframe strategy and market structure study.

ICT courses frequently explore these ideas, stressing the need to have a thorough grasp of the markets to create trading strategies. As a result, the logo functions as a visual summary of his lessons, signifying the breadth and depth of the information that ICT gives to his pupils. It serves as a beacon of guidance for individuals inside the "inner circle" and embodies the understanding of consumer behavior that Huddleston seeks to impart.

Michael J. Huddleston is a well-known person in the trading world, especially about Forex trading. He goes by the moniker Inner Circle Trader, or ICT. ICT is well-known for its extensive library of free instructional Forex trading materials, which encompasses a wide range of subjects linked to trading, including price movement, market structure, and psychological elements of trading. Huddleston presents himself as a teacher and mentor, offering in-depth information and tactics that can give traders an advantage in the financial sector.

His method integrates several technical analysis techniques with ideas like fractals, market sentiment, and Fibonacci ratios. He offers tactics that are meant to be more advanced than simple trading advice in his material, which delves deeper into the nuances of trading. The foundation of ICT's brand is exclusivity and cutting-edge insight, implying that individuals who study under him are privy to exclusive knowledge that holds the key to profitable trading.

Implementing ICT Strategies Into Practice for Improved Market Understanding

ICT strategy implementation calls for a thorough strategy. Traders gain the ability to recognize and analyze the goals and behaviors of institutional participants, which improves their ability to forecast market moves.

Making wise trading decisions requires an understanding of market structure, including trends, consolidation zones, and levels of support and resistance.

To accommodate diverse trading styles like intra-day, swing, or position trading, ICT techniques also make use of many periods to match trading actions with market dynamics. All things considered, ICT for trading provides a comprehensive and detailed view of the financial markets, helping traders successfully navigate and trade with greater proficiency.

ICT TRADING STRATEGY FOREX

ICT Components

The trading strategy known as "Inner Circle Trader" (ICT) focuses on comprehending market manipulation and structure to spot trading opportunities. Several essential components make up the ICT trading idea, including:

1. Market Structure: ICT traders start by examining the price movement and chart patterns that emerge from the actions of market participants. Finding critical support and resistance levels and the general trend direction of the market are the objectives.

2. Liquidity: Big traders, such as banks and institutions, usually place their orders in parts of the market that have high liquidity. This is where ICT traders search for these locations. For smaller traders looking to capitalize on the

liquidity these larger traders supply, these locations might present trading possibilities.

3. The belief held by many ICT traders is that major participants frequently influence the market to produce erroneous breakouts in addition to price fluctuations. To have an advantage in the market, they seek to uncover these manipulations.

4. Technical Analysis: To assess the market and spot trading opportunities, ICT traders employ technical analysis techniques including price movement, chart patterns, and indicators.

5. Risk Management: An essential component of the ICT trading idea is risk management. ICT traders prioritize protecting their money through prudent risk management, which includes position size and the use of stop-loss orders.

6. Trading Psychology: Lastly, ICT traders understand the significance of trading psychology to their trading performance. Their goal is to develop a patient and disciplined attitude that will enable them to properly control their emotions and remain focused on their trading approach.

All things considered, the ICT trading idea is a thorough method that integrates risk management, market structure research, and technical analysis to find and seize trading opportunities in the market.

Factors Affecting ICT Trading

Several factors can influence the success and efficiency of any trading strategy, including ICT trading, and these elements can differ from trader to trader.

Expertise and Experience: The effectiveness of any trading strategy is greatly influenced by the trader's degree of experience and expertise. A trader with greater expertise may be better equipped to adjust and make use of the ICT approach.

Market Conditions: The state of the market affects how effective any trading strategy is. A strategy that performs well in one set of market conditions might not be as successful in another.

Risk Management: A trader's capacity to effectively manage risk determines how successful a trading strategy will be in many cases. To succeed in trading over the long run, one must properly manage risk.

Flexibility: A sound trading strategy should be able to change with the movements of the market. Traders must have the flexibility to modify their plans in response to shifting market circumstances and trends.

Discipline and Patience: These qualities are necessary for every trading strategy. Applying the approach consistently and adhering to its principles is typically the key to success.

Constant Learning and Improvement: The most prosperous traders are those who never stop learning, evolving, and refining their approaches. They might combine several techniques, such as ICT components, to develop a customized and effective trading strategy.

Back-testing and Evaluation: To fully grasp the method's past performance, traders should carry out extensive backtesting and evaluation of the approach. This can shed light on potential

ICT TRADING STRATEGY FOREX

performance possibilities for the approach in various market situations.

Chapter 2: ICT Killzones

Meaning of ICT Killzone

The term "ICT (Inner Circle Trader) Killzones" describes discrete periods that are important to traders during the 24-hour FX trading cycle. The trader known only as "The Inner Circle Trader," who disseminates instructional materials on forex trading, is the source of the teachings and ideas employed in these periods.

Finding times during the trading day when there is a higher likelihood of market turns or a greater possibility of big liquidity moves is the concept underlying ICT Killzones. For traders who deal in the major currency pairings, these times are quite important.

When the market is more volatile and liquid during a certain part of the trading day, it's referred to as a "kill zone" in forex. Trading professionals might take advantage of this window of opportunity to profit on probable price swings. Historical data, market movements, and important support and resistance levels are usually analyzed to find kill zones.

To find the best entry and exit positions for their transactions, traders frequently employ kill zones. The ability to spot possible breakouts, reversals, or trend extensions allows traders to make well-informed trading decisions. This is achieved by keeping an eye on the market during these times of increased activity.

To further understand what a kill zone is, let's look at an example. Let's say a trader observes that there is a regular spike in volatility of the EUR/USD currency pair between 8:00 AM and 10:00 AM EST. The trader views this two-hour interval as the death zone for that particular currency pair. Concentrating on this time range may allow the trader to seize advantageous trading chances.

The Four ICT Killzones

The four main ICT Killzones are as follows:

The Asian Range Killzone

This includes the first few hours of the Asian trading day. Currently, there may be less liquidity, which allows traders to assess the range movement of the price.

The initial trading window in the forex market with the best combinations of the Australian dollar, New Zealand dollar, and Japanese yen is known as the "Asian kill zone." The US dollar often consolidates during this session since these are the most active pairings at this time.

The Asian kill zone is between 8:00 PM and 10:00 PM. During this time, the higher time frame bias is often beneficial; however, a bullish or bearish short-term retracement can also provide an excellent trade entry. Due to US Dollar consolidation during this timeframe, the majority of trade setups during this period occur in cross pairings. The Asian open often sets up an ideal trade entry pattern that may yield a scalp trade of 15-20 pip.

The London Open Killzone

The start of the London session, which is a major event in the world of forex trading, marks the activation of this Killzone. Numerous institutional traders enter the market at the opening, which might lead to significant price swings.

The London kill zone is where the London session opens and has the most trading activity compared to other sessions. During this time, the most popular pairings are the British pound (GBP) and the euro (EUR). The largest chance of a significant directional change in a day is observed in the London session.

Characteristics of London Killzone

Generally, the greater time frame bias is beneficial during the ICT London kill zone, which is between 2:00 AM to 5:00 AM.

- For the most part, the London Open sets up an ideal trade entry pattern that may provide directional trades with more than thirty pip gains.

- During London's kill zone on a bullish day, prices often reach the Asian high and then rise the next day.

- Bearish days in the London kill zone typically see price capture the Asian low and form the day's low before moving upward.

The New York Open Killzone

Similar to the London Open, there can be significant volatility at the beginning of the New York session. The United States' entry into the market can significantly influence price movements due to its crucial position in the FX arena.

The New York session opens at the ICT New York kill zone, and it is crucial to monitor and trade pairings that are paired with US dollars during this time.

Characteristics of New York Killzone

• The ICT New York Killzone is from 7:00 AM to 9:00 AM. During this time, the higher time frame inclination is often favorable, but a bullish or bearish short-term retracement can still provide an excellent trade entry.

Because the London and New York sessions overlap, the New York session is turbulent with high trading volume. • The New York session mainly retraces back to the London trading zone and sets up an ideal trade entry structure that can give 30–40 pip trades.

The London Close Killzone

This stage corresponds with the end of the London trading session. Major news events in Europe are often taken into account by the market at this point, which may cause trend variations or retractions.

ICT Killzones are frequently used by forex traders to hone their techniques by taking advantage of these potentially very liquid times. But like with any trading principle, it's important to use strict risk management and refrain from relying too much on one particular tactic. When the London session ends, the ICT London close kill zone is often a less volatile moment. The majority of the time, the price returns to its daily range, providing an ideal trading entry scenario. It is best to trade major pairs along with the US dollar at this time.

Characteristics of London Close Killzone

The time frame for ICT London's close kill zone is from 10:00 AM to 12:00 PM.

• A five-minute OTE setup with a 15–20 pip scalp trade is available in the London close kill zone.

• On a bullish day, following the day's high, prices retrace to the daily band during the London close kill zone.

• In the London close kill zone on a negative day, the price retraces back to the daily band after reaching the day's low.

Importance of ICT Killzones to Forex Traders

ICT Killzones identify times during the trading day when market activity and possible turnarounds are more likely. Knowing when these times are coming may help traders set themselves up for big changes in the market, whether they're brought on by greater liquidity or the entry or leave of key participants.

Identifying ICT Killzones

The London and New York periods offer the best trading chances since they are characterized by an inflow of institutional traders, which indicates possible price volatility.

Specifically, GMT+0 timings for Asia (00:00-05:00), London open (07:00-10:00), New York

(12:00-14:00), and London close (15:00-17:00) are needed for accurate kill zone charting. Finding these times of significant volatility requires the use of indicator characteristics such as showing London, Asian, and New York sessions, and Kill Zones.

To maximize market trend exploitation, the market behavior approach recommends that "Asia builds up, London alters, New York distributes," which directs trading within sessions.

- During the New York session, breakout possibilities are seen between 7 and 9 a.m. for noteworthy market moves and possible trend confirmations.

Crucial ICT Killzones include London and New York openings when an inflow of institutional

ICT TRADING STRATEGY FOREX

traders indicates possible price volatility and breakout possibilities.

●Killzone expertise entails realizing the value of Asian, London Open, New York, and London Close settings, which provide traders with a time edge.

●Trader activity is strongest in the London session during Killzone, suggesting tremendous implementation interest and the possibility of large gains.

Optimization and Risk Management

Managing risk entails determining whether to take profits based on individual risk-reward ratios and taking early morning market volatility—particularly during the New York sessions—into account.

ICT TRADING STRATEGY FOREX

Order placement makes use of the dynamics of the London Kill Zone to enable strategic entrance; orders are placed at pivotal points in anticipation of liquidity sweeps. Confirming reversals at critical junctures in the London Kill Zone and coordinating actions with the dynamics of the market and session constitute strategy confirmation.

Chapter 3: Order Flow

Order Flow Trading: What is It?

An approach to trading known as "order flow trading" involves defining trade edges by examining publicized and/or executed orders. Order flow traders try to make money by taking advantage of instabilities in the market.

Order flow trading is a form of technical analysis whereby future price movement is predicted by observing the movement of trade orders and their consequent influence on the market. To put it another way, you may observe how other market players are making trades (buying or selling) by using the order flow analysis.

Order flow analysis and tape reading are other names for order flow trading.

You may identify the last specifics of the volume of purchases and sales with the aid of order flow analysis. It's an in-depth analysis of candlestick research. Order flow analysis may be used to examine the wealth of information contained in each candlestick.

Order flow trading, to put it simply, is a kind of trading that focuses on comprehending how traders' choices cause orders to enter the market.

Order flow trading is not a novel approach to trading the forex markets; rather, it has been there since the first days of the modern financial markets, but not in the configuration that is familiar to us now.

Order flow refers to how buy and sell orders would 'flow' in the market when various market players make choices connected to trading, such as placing trades, closing transactions, and realizing gains.

The Difference Between Order Flow Trading And Other Types Of Trading

To help people understand exactly what order flow trading entails and doesn't when it comes to topics like price action trading, I think it's vital to briefly go over the distinctions between order flow trading and other forms of trading.

In that both order flow trading and price action trading advocate a particular approach to market analysis, they are comparable forms of trading. Order flow traders think they can forecast the direction of the market by just watching the traders' movements, whereas price action traders think they can anticipate the market's movement by looking at the price of the market.

If you were to ask me what kind of trader I think I am, I would say that I think of myself as a hybrid of the two because I use order flow trading knowledge along with the standard tools that price action traders use, such as Fibonacci retracements, support and resistance levels, and pin bars. For instance, I can predict when a pin bar is going to emerge because I understand order flow trading, which helps me identify when bank traders take gains off of their trades.

How Does Order Flow Trading Work?

The theory behind order flow trading is that you can predict the direction of the market movement with a high degree of accuracy if you know when and where traders are likely to make their trading choices. This is because every action a trader makes—whether to open, close, or otherwise—puts an order into the market that might result in a price change. A price adjustment can only be effected by thousands of orders entering the market at once; a single order cannot influence the price.

An order flow trader's primary objective is to comprehend how other market participants trade since doing so will enable him to predict when a sizable number of orders will likely enter the market and drive price movements.

These days, it might be challenging to figure out how other traders trade, mostly because there are so many various trading methods available. Fortunately, we don't have to be aware of the intricacies of the trading methods individuals employ.

We can determine the time and location of their decision-making process, which will involve placing orders into the market, by simply understanding the fundamental objective of their trading strategy.

Trader types in the forex market mostly employ two kinds of trading strategies:

Strategies for trend trading and reversals

Trading methods that follow trends and those that reverse trends.

The objective of trend trading methods is to position the trader to take a position in the market after a shift has happened. An excellent illustration of this is a moving average system, in which the averages only intersect after the market has moved up or down for a while.

Currently, the objective of a reverse trading technique is to enter the transaction before the market moves. Reversal trading tactics include but are not limited to, identifying candlestick patterns in supply and demand zones or trading at support and resistance levels. Even though the two techniques are very different from each other, they are identical in that they both try to enter the trader before the market has moved.

Thus, while there are many other tactics for trend trading and reversal trading available, they are all essentially variations on the same theme.

Either before or after a shift has occurred, they are attempting to persuade a trader to enter the market. You may avoid learning about the nuances of any trading strategy by just knowing these two facts, which will let you know when traders who employ these techniques are most likely to join the market and place their trades.

Basics of Order Flow Trading

Now, let's quickly review some of the fundamental order flow ideas that you will need to know if you plan to use order flow analysis to trade the forex market.

Recognizing How Various Orders Affect Market Pricing

Even though various traders' trading decisions ultimately affect the price, the orders that are placed into the market as a result of these decisions are ultimately what drive up and down movements in the market price. Being an order flow trader requires you to grasp what these orders are and the various impacts they have on the market price. This will help you comprehend why the market moves in the ways that it does.

In the market, traders can execute two distinct kinds of orders. These two orders, when executed, have distinct impacts on the market price and are performed by traders for different purposes.

Let's look at what these directives mean.

Market Orders

When a trader wants to get a deal into the market as quickly as possible, they will utilize a market order. A trader is going to utilize a market order to initiate a trade to ensure he does not miss out on an opportunity to earn money immediately when he sees anything occurring on his charts that he considers as a chance to do so. Reactive trading techniques are those in which the trader enters a transaction using a market order given that the trader is responding to what he observes is happening in the market at that moment.

Pending Order / Limit Order

Traders who wish to place a trade at a price that hasn't been achieved in the market might utilize pending orders or limit orders. These traders prefer to place their deals at a later time rather than immediately, as do others who use market orders. Because they ensure you are going to purchase or sell currencies at a price the market hasn't yet reached, stop losses are also known as limit orders.

Using a market order with a stop loss to enter a trade is equivalent to placing two orders into the market because the stop loss is a limit order to sell or buy at a price that hasn't been reached. Trading strategies that use a limit order to enter a trade are called predictive because the trader has placed the order at a price where they anticipate a future event to occur. The primary distinction that exists between market orders and pending / limit orders remains the impact they have on the market price. Market liquidity is reduced once a market order is placed, whereas market liquidity is increased when a pending or limited order is put in.

Advantages of Using Order Flow Strategy

Utilizing the order flow trading strategy has several advantages, such as providing valuable insights into market participants' activity, accurately identifying possible trade setups, and identifying the best times to enter and leave the market based on order flow data analysis.

Chapter 4: Fair Value Gap

FX Fair Value Gap

In the world of Forex trading, a Fair Value Gap (FVG) occurs when a currency pair's price moves solely in one direction and exits a certain level when trading activity is lower. When used with order blocks, Fvg might offer fresh trading chances.

Price increases resulting from unequal forces on buyers and sellers are known as fair value gaps. Sometimes these differences are referred to as Price Value Gaps, Singles, or imbalances. The term "fair value gap" (also known as "FVG") will be used in this book.

When the supply of buyers is substantially greater or lesser than the demand of sellers, a fair value gap is present in the market. A fast shift in an instrument's price in the direction of increased supply or decreased demand may result from this. This sharp price movement's location on the chart is then shown by the Fair Value Gap. Market imbalances or inefficiencies are referred to as fair value gaps, and they are most frequently employed by price action traders. All these "imbalances" are saying is that there is a disparity between purchasing and selling.

Measuring Fair Value Gap

Apart from Breakaway Gaps, another important idea in the field of Forex trading is called "Measuring Fair Value Gap." It has a special function in examining market dynamics and is generated in response to a fair value gap. One characteristic that distinguishes the Measuring Fair Value Gap is its tendency to stay open. Its endurance arises from the strong institutional order flow that frequently envelops it and drives prices steadily in one direction.

Consequently, there is a lower chance of the Measuring Gap closing. Serving as a signal of the institutional order flow in a certain direction is its main function. The appearance of the Bearish Measuring Fair Value Gap indicates a predominately bearish order flow in the market. On the contrary, a bullish measuring gap suggests that there is a bullish order flow in place.

This significant institutional order flow is the primary cause of the Measuring Gap's propensity to stay open. Institutions frequently execute big orders that force the market to move strongly in one direction, giving little opportunity for a price reversal. To sum up, traders may effectively identify and analyze institutional order flow by utilizing the Measuring Fair Value Gap. Its tenacity and focus offer insightful information about the general attitude of the market, helping traders make wise choices.

How Fair Value Gap Forms

It is not by chance that there is a Fair Value Gap when the market price differs from the average. Consequently, we outline the conditions under which an FVG is likely to arise below.

Significant occurrences

An abrupt shift in market mood due to significant news might result in an FVG. One example of such news would be an unanticipated rise in interest rates. An FVG might ensue from this rise if there is a surge in the native currency. Numerous things might happen that will change the market significantly. Along with macroeconomic information, these also include political headlines, such as details about the start of hostilities, earthquakes, and other natural disasters.

The announcement of business financial performance

Additionally, there is going to be a quick change in price if a firm releases significantly unexpected findings. The price of the stock index, of which the firm is a component, may then reflect this and constitute the FVG.

Substantial institutional transactions

FVGs can result from large institutional deals as well. A market gap may arise, for instance, if a sizable hedge fund purchases a sizable number of shares. Additionally, if a central bank begins to purchase or sell native currency on the market, among other interventions.

How to Trade the Fair Value Gap

Frequently, Fair Value Gaps fill up since these gaps indicate an imbalance. With this information, we can locate the ideal entry point for a trade with accuracy.

Covering the void

It's critical to ascertain the current trend while employing this method. One better time scale to determine this should be daily, weekly, or H4. Lower highs (LH) and lower lows (LL) are the results of a downtrend, whereas higher highs (HH) and higher lows (HL) are the results of a healthy upswing. A break of structure (BOS) is created and the trend is probably going to continue if the Higher High breaks in an uptrend or the Lower Low breaks in a downtrend.

A change of character (CHOCH) happens when an uptrend breaks HL and moves to the downside, increasing the likelihood that the uptrend will reverse and begin to collapse. When the market is in a downtrend, the comparison is inverted, meaning that there is a greater possibility of a market rise than a market decrease when the lower high (LH) is broken to the upside.

Places at which the BOS or CHOCH break happens should be noted. Should the break be followed by the creation of an FVG, the market is projected to keep heading in the course of the FVG that generated the break, indicating a powerful, impulsive move. In this scenario, a patient trader would watch for the point at which the broken line returns, filling the gap that opened on it, and then think about making an entry on the filled gap. Less probability exists for the gap to function as support (uptrend) or resistance (downtrend) if the break happens so that the break line is outside the gap.

Advantages and Disadvantages of Fair Value Gap

Advantages:

● Trading FVG allows a trader to get a favorable risk/reward ratio.

● FVG is visible on a chart.

- A vast range of assets, such as equities, commodities, and currencies, can be traded using this technique.

- It functions in all time intervals.

Disadvantages:

- Gaps may not always fill or may occasionally be "overshot." Uncertainty may result from this.

- FVGs are a type of liquidity that smart money has amassed. As a result, the price may occasionally move sharply in the reverse path of the gap.

Additional Tips For Fair Value Gap

Use several indicators: Using many indicators might be helpful while trading FVG. One useful tool is our Purple Gap indicator, for instance.

ICT TRADING STRATEGY FOREX

●utilize stop losses: One important tip for trading FVG is to always utilize stop losses. This will lessen your losses and safeguard your gains.

●Await Confirmation: It is crucial to hold off on making a trade until you have proof that the market will move forward in the course of the gap following the filling of the FVG.

●The timing.

●Liquidity Pick: Either be patient for liquidity to get selected if the gap is at an area where it might be picked (for instance, if the FVG is close to the high or low of the prior day). Proceed with the trade only after that.

Chapter 5: Change of Character CHoCH

A Change of Character, or ChoCh for short, is essentially the first order flow change in a financial market. When a small supply or demand zone breaks, a possible change in the market trend is indicated, and this structural shift takes place. It frequently indicates the possibility of a short- or even long-term asset, equity, or currency reversal.

All things considered, ChoCh is a useful trend reversal form for traders looking to pinpoint times when the market's usual behavior changes. It's similar to identifying the minute indications of a shifting wind direction before a storm.

How to Use ChoCh in Trading

It may be seen on any trading platform and at any point in time. It can therefore be used for a variety of purposes. However, these numerous applications eventually fall under two primary categories:

- ChoCh - Higher time frame,

- ChoCh - Lower Timeframe

To see the larger picture, use ChoCh on longer timescales. It assists traders in determining the general direction of the market and identifying any major reversals. You may more effectively match your holdings with the emotion of the market by identifying a ChoCh changeover.

Conversely, traders use ChoCh to detect possible trading opportunities and make well-informed decisions when evaluating lower timeframes, like the 1-minute timeframe. This methodical analysis helps traders identify short-term changes in order flow, which enables them to make accurate trade entries. With this knowledge, traders can modify their strategies, control risk, and latch onto profitable opportunities.

How to Identify ChoCh

A careful examination of market trends and indicators is necessary to spot a change in character. Important indicators include:

•Break down of trend lines: A ChoCh may be indicated by a distinct break through a key trend line.

- Volume spike: A sudden jump in trade volume that coincides with a price change may indicate a possible change in character.

- Candlestick patterns: Particular patterns, such as an engulfing or doji candle, might indicate a change in the emotion of the market.

Forex trading requires a tactical approach to execution as well as a detailed comprehension of market signals to use the Change of Character (ChoCh) idea. The following are some efficient ways for traders to use ChoCh in the FX market:

Market analysis: Start by doing a comprehensive examination of the currency market. Examine broad patterns in significant currency pairings that may be getting close to important levels of support or resistance. ChoCh frequently appears

ICT TRADING STRATEGY FOREX

close to these critical junctures, suggesting a possible change in the direction of the market.

1. Recognize ChoCh signals: The main ways to identify ChoCh are through volume and price activity. Change of Character may be indicated by an abrupt and notable price movement that deviates from the current trend, particularly when volume spikes coincide with the movement. concentrate on candlestick patterns. A bearish reversal may be indicated by a massive bearish engulfing candle that closes an uptrend (ChoCh).

2. Verification: It's important to use other technical indicators to corroborate the ChoCh signal. This might be the moving averages beginning to flatten or reverse direction, the Relative Strength Index (RSI) deviating from the price movement or other indicators of

diminishing momentum. Trading choices have a more solid foundation when they are based on confirmation, which helps weed out erroneous signals.

3. Carefully consider your entry and departure places when a ChoCh has been verified. If the price falls below a recent low and the ChoCh signals a bearish reversal, you might want to consider going short. However, a price breakthrough above a previous high indicates a positive turnaround. If you think the market could move differently than you expected, place stop-loss orders just past the moment of reversal to reduce your possible losses.

Chapter 6: Risk Management and Control

Risk management: While trading on ChoCh signals, effective risk control is essential. Because of this, you should utilize a cautious leverage ratio and modify the size of your position based on the amount of risk you are ready to accept. This is because markets are volatile by nature and may reverse course quickly.

ICT Forex Trading: Avoid Common Errors and Maximize Profitability

Foreign currency trading, or forex trading, has become extremely popular in recent years. It provides people with the chance to profit from changes in currency values. However, forex trading has its own set of difficulties and traps, just like any other type of investing. I will look at a few typical ICT forex trading errors in this part and offer advice on how to increase profits.

1. Insufficient knowledge and education

Entering the market unprepared and ignorant is among some of the biggest blunders novices in forex trading make. Without a firm grasp of the basics, traders run the risk of making expensive errors in the complicated and extremely volatile world of forex trading. Devoting time to acquiring knowledge about forex trading is vital, encompassing technical and fundamental analysis, risk mitigation, and trading tactics.

2. Trading from an emotional standpoint

In forex trading, emotions can cause one's judgment to be impaired. Fear and greed can cause traders to act rashly and go off course from their trading strategy. Since emotional traders frequently follow trends or hastily sell when markets are weak, emotional trading frequently ends in losses. To prevent making irrational trading decisions, one must adopt a disciplined strategy. This entails establishing precise entry and exit locations, observing stop-loss orders, and sticking to a precise trading strategy.

3. Overtrading

One typical mistake made by forex traders, particularly novices, is overtrading. It alludes to overtrading motivated by the need to turn a profit quickly. Because traders may initiate deals without sufficient research or reason, overtrading frequently results in poor decision-making. Exhaustion and large losses may ensue from this. It's critical to have a clear trading strategy with precise entry and exit criteria to prevent overtrading. Traders ought to prioritize quality above number while making transactions.

4. A lack of self-control and patience

Forex trading calls for self-control and patience. Profitable traders are aware that losses are unavoidable and that not every deal will become a profit. It's critical to follow the trading strategy and ignore transient market swings. Waiting for the ideal trade opportunities to present themselves also calls for patience. Impetuous trading might result in unfavorable outcomes and lost chances.

5. Disregarding Risk Management

Despite being important, risk management in forex trading is frequently disregarded by traders. Placing stop-loss orders to restrict possible losses, varying the portfolio, and investing a fair portion of cash in each transaction are all components of effective risk management. Also, traders ought to refrain from taking on more risk than they can bear to lose. Through the application of efficient risk management techniques, traders may safeguard their funds and lessen the consequences of losses.

Increasing Earnings in ICT Forex Trading

The main objective of forex trading is to maximize profits, even though avoiding frequent errors is vital. The following advice can help increase profitability:

1. Constant Learning: Because the forex markets are ever-changing, it's critical to keep current on the newest trends and advancements. Traders ought to devote time to ongoing education, webinars, financial news reading, and trend analysis.

2. Backtesting Strategies: It is a good idea to use historical data to backtest a trading strategy before putting it into practice. This enables traders to assess the strategy's effectiveness and make any required modifications before risking real money.

3. Money Management: Long-term prosperity depends on the application of sound money management strategies. To minimize risk on a

ICT TRADING STRATEGY FOREX

single trade, traders need to ascertain the proper risk-reward ratio for every deal.

4. Technology Utilization: Profitability may be greatly increased by utilizing technology. To increase trade execution efficiency and seize market opportunities, traders might employ trading software, algorithms, and automated trading systems.

To sum up,

Though it does not come without difficulties, ICT forex trading presents a significant opportunity for financial gain. A trader's chances of success can be increased by steering clear of typical mistakes including emotional trading, under-education, overtrading, and disregarding risk management. Increasing profitability also requires focused trading, ongoing education, and

ICT TRADING STRATEGY FOREX

sound money management. By possessing the appropriate information, abilities, and mentality, traders may effectively traverse the forex market and realize their financial objectives.

www.ingramcontent.com/pod-product-compliance
Lightning Source LLC
Chambersburg PA
CBHW070413230526
45471CB00006B/2790